Alois Podhajsky

The White Stallions of Vienna

Translated
by Frances Hogarth-Gaute
and Eva Podhajsky

The Sportsman's Press
London

First published in Great Britain 1963
This edition published by The Sportsman's Press in 1985

© 1962 Nymphenburger Verlagshandlung GmbH., München
English translation © Harrap Ltd.
Additional English translation © The Sportsman's Press

British Library Cataloguing in Publication Data

Podhajsky, Alois
    The White Stallions of Vienna.
    1. Spanische Reitschule—History
    I. Title   II. Frances Hogarth-Gaute and Eva Podhajsky   III. Triumph
    der Lipizzaner. *English*
    798.2′3′071043613   SF310.A953V53

    ISBN 0-948253-03-7

Printed in Austria

CONTENTS

Introduction

It is with great pleasure that I present this revised edition in a new format, of my husband's book of photographs illustrating the history, training and performance of the Lipizzaners.

May it introduce a new generation of readers to the miracle of the white stallions.

Eva Podhajsky

The old imperial city of Vienna, surviving all the chaos of the centuries, wars and revolutions, has remained a treasure-house of Western tradition, a nursery of the arts, a soil in which a feeling for antiquity mingles with a healthy sense of the present. Countless monuments of a great history and culture still speak today in a language that can be understood by Austrians and foreigners alike. Whether visitors read up their Baedeker before they visit Vienna or allow themselves to be led by the *genius loci* they cannot fail to come upon one unique piece of the living past, an example of baroque that irresistibly attracts and enthrals even modern man: the Spanish Riding School in the Hofburg, where the world-famous Lipizzaner horses show their exquisite skill today, as they have done for more than two hundred years.

Whoever attends the festive exhibitions of classic horsemanship in the light, lofty hall in the Michaelerplatz will certainly never forget the triumph of the Lipizzaner, the fluid, dancing movements of the aristocratic stallions in the controlled display of their great strength, the magnificent leaps, the *Pas de Trois*, and the graceful quadrille ballet. The present Riding Hall was completed between 1729 and 1735, and with its unsurpassed architecture provides the background for the formal, inspired interplay of man and animal. This Riding Hall, the creation of Fischer von Erlach, has witnessed a great deal of turbulent history, and when during World War II the city of Vienna was severely damaged the building was shaken to its foundations, but by good fortune avoided destruction, so it has been possible for an imperial tradition to be continued without interruption. In former centuries splendid ceremonies and gay receptions predominated; in our time equestrian skill, the delight of all who watch it, has taken their place.

And the Lipizzaner! These proud and noble white stallions! Their high intelligence and exceptional talent are already obvious during training. It is a pleasure to work with these clever horses, and it is easy to understand why the great masters of the Spanish Riding School are so passionately devoted to them and so full of praise for their qualities. Hardly another single breed of horse combines such individuality with receptiveness and obedience. In every era, therefore, new masters of equitation have always been found to cherish the property entrusted to them. Without slavishly following any particular plan, they have improved on tradition and skill, in the same way as artists constantly introduce new lines and features into traditional designs. Even those who have no real feeling for the finer points of dressage, constantly harking back to tradition in all its details and allusions, which seem to be borrowed from the dancing of an elegant era, and those to whom the fine distinction of breed is not yet obvious from the nobility of the horses' movements, cannot fail to have an instinctive feeling for equestrian perfection.

Riding with the Lipizzaner stands for elegance and skill. What lies behind it each man must discover for himself. But the effect of the performances, art created in time and space, might be lost if it could not be portrayed in a picture to be perfectly preserved in the memory. This desire to give permanence to the ephemeral is the reason for this book. The complete programme of the oldest riding school in the world, the only official home of classic riding, is reproduced in its pages. Here can be seen views from the galleries and boxes of the brilliant performances in Fischer von Erlach's Riding Hall. In this carefully chosen series of pictures the life of the silvery horses is traced back to their youth in the stud, through their everyday existence. We see the historic stud on the Karstplateau of Lipizza, the crowd of young stallions in the paddocks, their prancing and leaping in unrestrained pleasure, which prepare them for the realities of a horse's life. Then schooling begins under the direction of a dressage expert.

Engravings and photographs show the development of the classic equestrian art and portray the famous Viennese academy in its beginnings and at the height of its brilliant reputation. They trace the fate of the School through the perilous years of World War II, pick out the quiet work done behind the scenes, and accompany riders and horses on their festival tours all over the world. Prominent visitors are shown meeting the Lipizzaner.

The book is so planned that the reader sees only such pictures and subjects as represent in themselves and in their sequence the original spirit of classic horsemanship. Everything leads up to the perfect harmony of the great School ballet that can still be seen every Sunday beneath the crystal chandeliers of the baroque hall: the triumph of the white stallions of Vienna.

Exhibitions of Classical Horsemanship: Part I

Priceless crystal chandeliers sparkle like hundreds of candles, bathing the magnificent hall in enchanting splendour. The clear notes of a gay overture are heard, and in measured step eight riders in traditional dress appear on snow-white horses and salute.

The performance
begins . . .

The start of the *Pas de Trois*, a graceful dance on horseback. The swift, rhythmic movements are precisely timed to harmonize with the notes of a Mozart symphony – in fluid changes from open order to close grouping, performed by outstanding riders on perfectly trained School horses.

Colonel Podhajsky on Maestoso Alea, Oberbereiter Irbinger on Conversano Plutona, Bereiter Riedler on Conversano Benvenuta.

The young Lipizzaner stallions are so graceful and clever, so reliable and eager in character and temperament, that even the novices in the School can take part in the performances. As young, inexperienced remounts they often show signs of great talent.

All the paces and turns of the *haute école* consist of a complex series of attractive movements and figures, carried out by stallions at different stages of training in the various gaits and in waltz and march tempo.

"Work in Hand" is a preparation for the most difficult lessons, which are then executed with riders: advanced training that has become a fascinating art form in itself. To melodious chamber music Pluto Brezia rises to his full height helped by his instructor, and with a mighty thrust leaps almost upright in the *courbette*, while Neapolitano Santuzza, firmly held and encouraged by his master, completes a sublime *capriole*.

Visiting the Stallions in their Stables

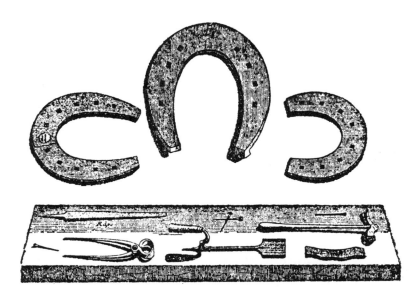

Before they appear in public artists of this class need leisure in comfortable surroundings.

The Stallburg in the heart of the city has, since 1565, been the regular Vienna home of the Lipizzaner and of the Imperial horses. It is enclosed by the towering Arkadenhof, which, like a well-built old palace, shuts out the sounds of everyday life.

The stallions are splendidly housed in roomy horse-boxes and
stalls decorated with stucco and clean as a new pin.

President Urho Kaleva Kekkonen of Finland shows great interest as he makes his round of the stalls, accompanied by Colonel Alois Podhajsky.

Very knowledgeably, Queen Elizabeth II visits the Lipizzaner stallions in their stables. Framed name-plates on the posts mark each stallion's stall, and the names of their sires and dams show their aristocratic origin.

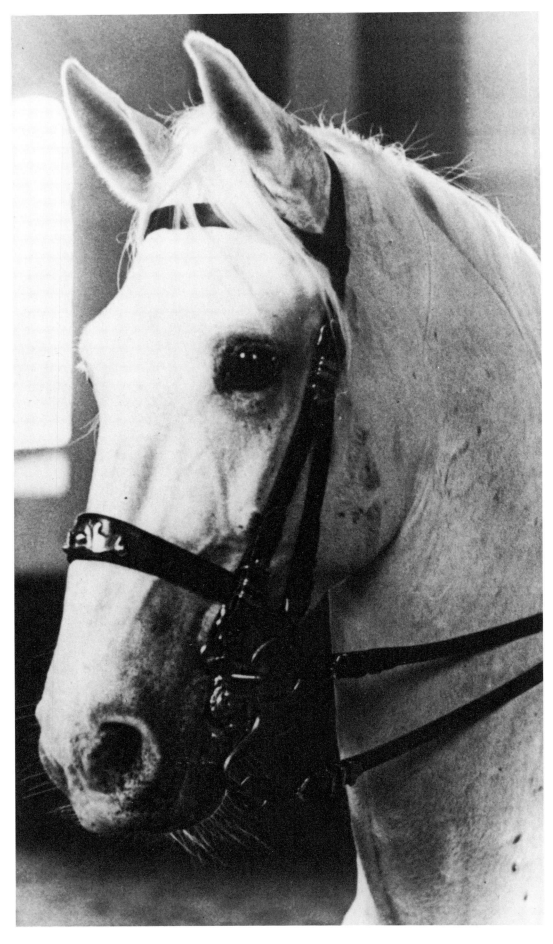

Here in honourable retirement lives a much travelled and world-famous master of the *haute école* – Pluto Theodorosta.

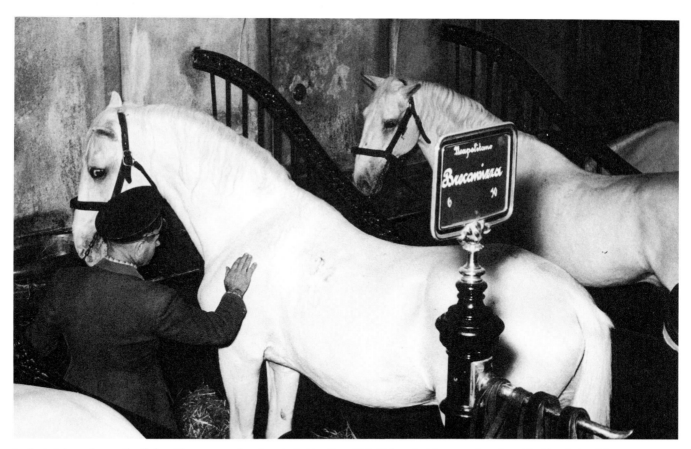

In their leisure hours the School horses receive devoted attention. It is fitting that horses of such noble blood should eat their hay from marble cribs.

Favory Kitty waits for his meal with well-bred patience.

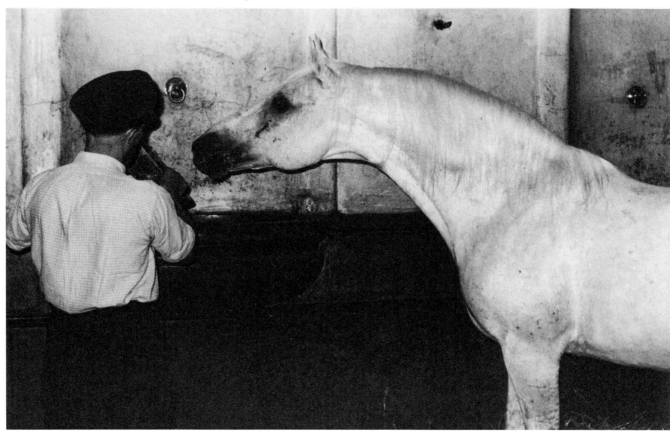

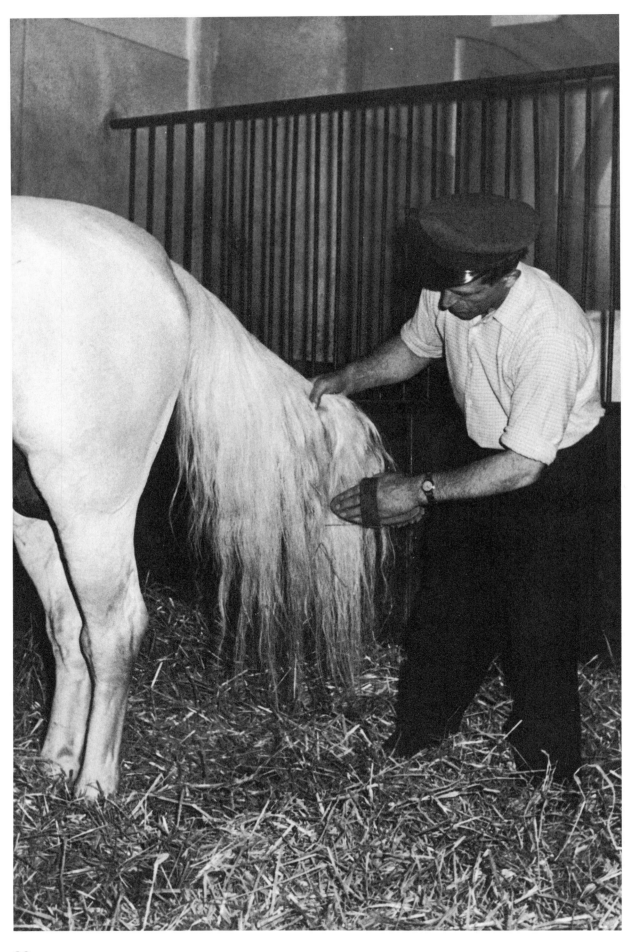

The silky tails always
get the best possible
attention.

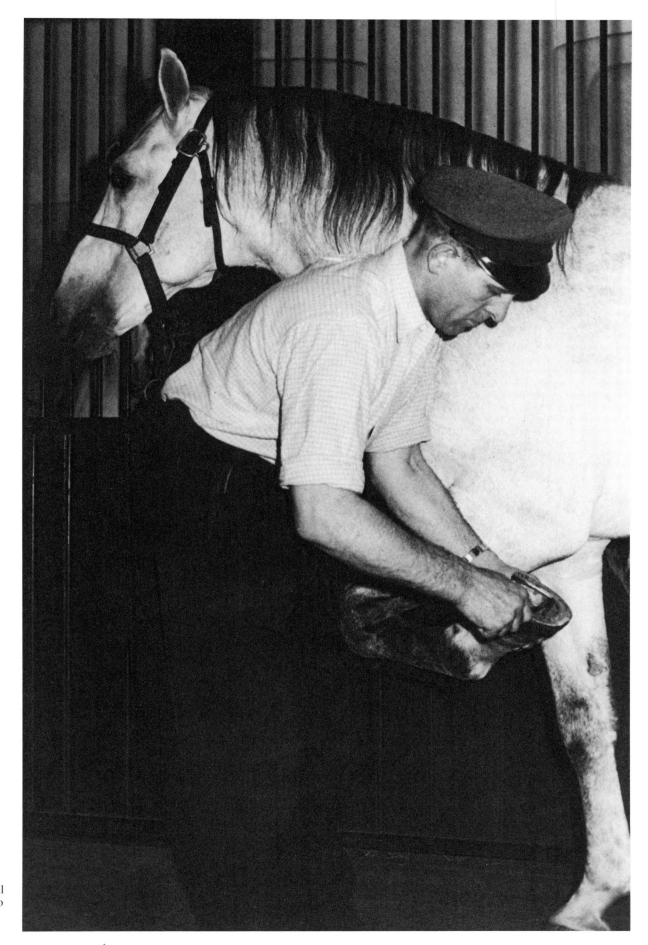

Regular and careful
attention is given to
the cleaning of the
hoofs and shoes.

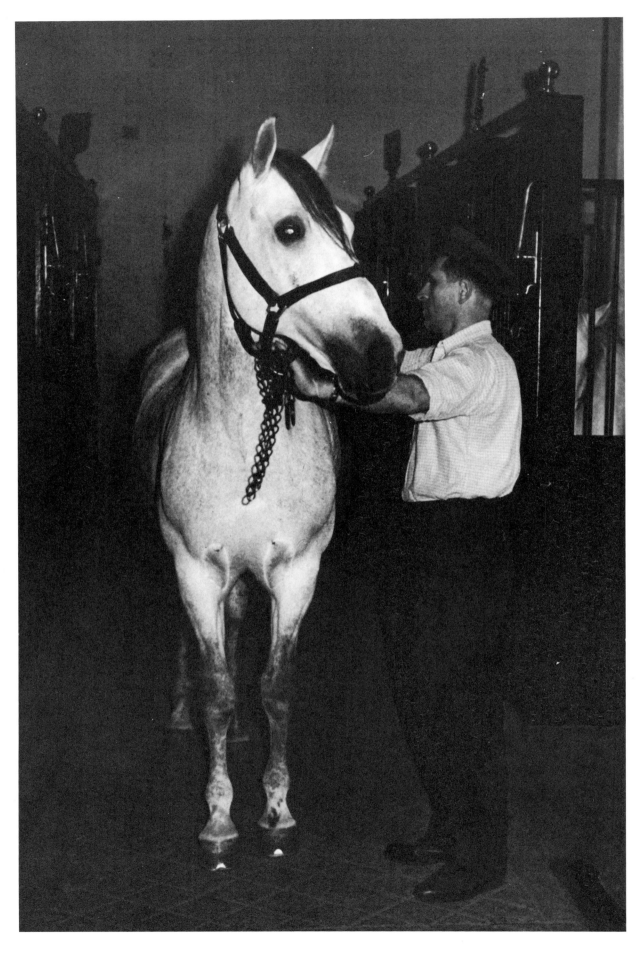

Daily grooming not only contributes to physical well-being, but also increases the horse's trust in the human beings around him.

Youthful Years
in the Stud

Before the stallions learn in traditional manner the seriousness of a horse's life by precisely ordered service in the Riding School in Vienna, they enjoy a happy and carefree youth in the stud – as offspring of a race that matures late and lives a long time.

Tired of frolicking, the foals nibble at the paddock fence and survey the passers-by.

In the morning the foals stream out joyously with the mares into the alluring green meadows, their dark young coats providing a lively contrast with the whiteness of their mothers'. As evening draws on they trot along in the middle of the herd, stupid with weariness, back to their stables.

The young mares, as formerly in Lipizza, have to undergo a thorough training between the shafts before they join the foaling mares.

Originating in the Karst mountains near Trieste, the Lipizzaner breed was transferred in 1919 to the old Austrian national stud at Piber near Graz, in Upper Styria.
Around the castle and church in Piber a strong thoroughbred stud herd thrives in lush green pasture.

Throughout the summer the young colts run free and grow up in the fresh mountain air on the high pastures of the Stubalpe and Brendlalm, while the mares amble slowly and with dignity over the green expanse, and the half-grown stallions size each other up with arched necks and mounting excitement, and even face humans with great self-possession.

Out of the shy, inquisitive horse-child there quickly emerges a bully spoiling for a fight, who seeks his fellows to romp about in wild games and youthful trials of strength with snapping teeth and flailing hoofs. This pushing, prancing, leaping, and turning reveals the first signs of great technical skill, which will be refined into true art through regular training in Vienna. Mastery then qualifies the élite among the stallions to return to the stud for the survival of the breed.

In a gentle but austere landscape stands a group of buildings of the manor type with gentlemen's houses and agricultural implements – and with horses and still more horses. Here, in 1580, the Lipizzaner breed of white horses was founded with Spanish bloodstock and the purity of the strain has been maintained through the centuries, so justifying the retention of the name of its place of origin.
The Royal Lipizza stud about the year 1700. A historic picture in the possession of the Spanish Riding School in Vienna.

Water in the high Karst is often short. When the horses return home to the old stables from pasture in the light scrub, mares and foals like to linger and take long draughts from the inexhaustible pond.

Stallions of today and their Ancestors

Founded in 1580 in the Karst stud with bloodstock of Spanish-Oriental origin, the Lipizzaner strain was strengthened and increased until the beginning of the eighteenth century with continuous supplies of similar blood, and later also through purchases from the Orient. The Arab and Barbary horses having already stood sponsors to the old Iberian horses, the Spanish element is still predominant in the Lipizzaner breed even today.

The question is often asked whether the School stallions of today reveal in their faces their descent in the sire's line from Pluto, Conversano or Neapolitano, or from Favory, Maestoso or Siglavy. It is often supposed that this should be recognizable, but this is not the case, since, both from the dam's side and from the dams of all their fore-fathers, other strains are united in the descendants.

Siglavy Monterosa shows his heritage from Oriental forebears in the fine sculpture and noble outlines clearly discernible under the skin of his clever head.

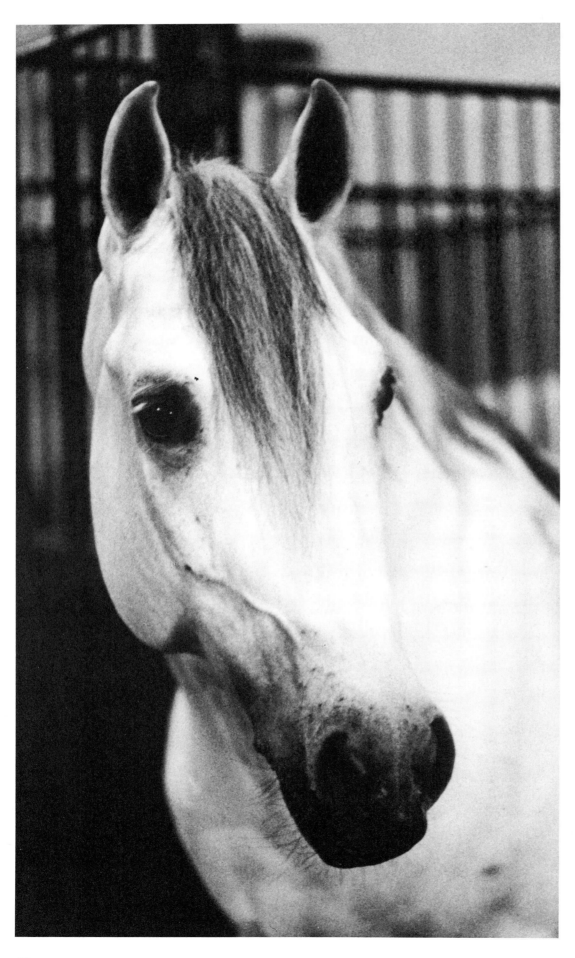

Facing each other, showing the Arab contours at their best, are Neapolitano Albina and Siglavy Bona, quite typical Lipizzaner. Equally so is the maturer Conversano Plutona with his harsher lines.

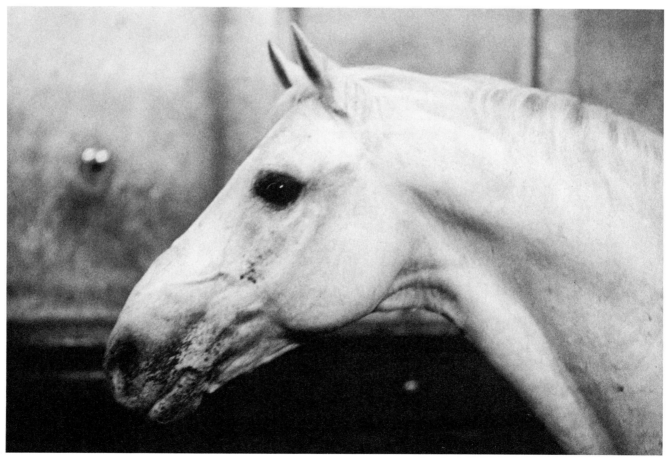

Bona
1881
Favory Sesana

Bona, karster
1875
Neapolitano Mahonia

Bona, karster
1856
Gazlan, Orig. Arab.

Bona, karster
1838
Siglavy Africa, karster

Primavera, karster
1829
Forester, Arab.

Bellafiglia III, koptschaner
1820
Lipp, koptschaner

Bellafiglia, koptschaner
1808
Maestoso Virtuosa, karster

Romana II
1882
Ben Azet, Arab.

Romana, karster
1871
Samson, Orig. Arab.

Romana, karster
1854
Gazlan, Orig. Arab.

Romana, karster
1833
Kohejl, Hollihock, Angl. Arab.

Sardinia, karster
1827
Maestoso Grozana, karster

Plutona IV, karster
1815
Vezir, Arab.

Plutona, koptschaner
1801
Pluto, karster

Amorosa, kladruber
1792
Sanspareil

Presciana
1782
Kladruberin.

One of the pedigrees in beautiful handwriting, kept for more than ninety years, shows at once how frequently the various ancestors are linked in later generations.

The leopard stallion Papagallo, painted by an unknown artist in a completely natural manner, looks nimble like a ballet-dancer.

Portraits of noble stallions in idealized landscapes by George Hamilton, products of trained observation and delicate brushwork, decorate the reception rooms of the Spanish Riding School in Vienna, providing pictorial documentary proof of the dark colouring which used to be much commoner.

Black horse with four white socks: Cerbero in the *capriole*, 1717.

55

A bay Spaniard in the *piaffe*, 1720.

The Evolution of Classical Horsemanship

There were rules for riders even in ancient days, and thanks to the devotion of the philologists a set of riding instructions has actually survived, compiled by no less a person than Xenophon, the great general, statesman, historiographer, and pupil of Socrates. The basic themes of his work *On Equitation*, dating from about 400 B.C., are still valid today. He has described very poetically the aims of riding: "On horses such as these even gods and heroes will appear, and men who know how to work well with them look magnificent."

With the decline of ancient culture the art of horsemanship deteriorated. It was revived in Renaissance Italy about two thousand years after its zenith and, like the fine arts, equitation flourished, and special riding academies were instituted. Using Xenophon's work as a basis, the nobleman Federigo Grisone, hailed by his contemporaries as "the Father of Equitation," excited particularly wide interest in Naples through his active practical teaching and the publication in 1552 of his *Ordini di Cavalcare*, which pointed the way. His choice of methods of mastering the horse did not preclude force.

Equestrian groups from the Parthenon frieze. Reliefs from the School of Phidias.

Wie das Füllen auß dem gestüd zufü-
ren / vnd etzliche tag zam vnd gehorsam
zumachen.

C iij

This illustration, which shows how to bring remounts from the stud into the riding stables and get them used to being there, would be hard to beat for drastic measures. Woodcut from *Ordini di Cavalcare.*

60

From some fifty curbs recommended by Master Grisone as being suitable for a "gentle, good mouth" it is easy to see that he was decidedly not squeamish. Woodcut from *Ordini di Cavalcare*.

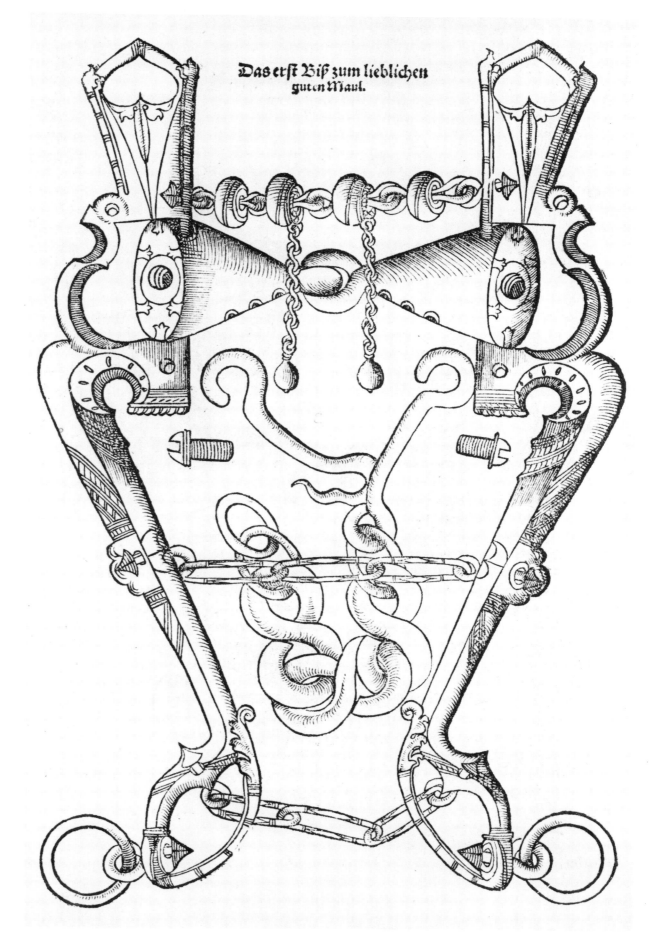

Das erst Biß zum lieblichen guten Maul.

The revival of horsemanship soon spread from the Neapolitan schools to France, where Antoine de Pluvinel, the Royal Equerry, practised teaching methods he had learned in Italy, but in a noticeably refined form, carrying them further and enriching them with pillar work. The essence of his teaching was set down in the form of a dialogue between the king and his riding master and was published under the title *Manège du Roi*, in 1623, some years after his death, and illustrated with fine copper engravings.

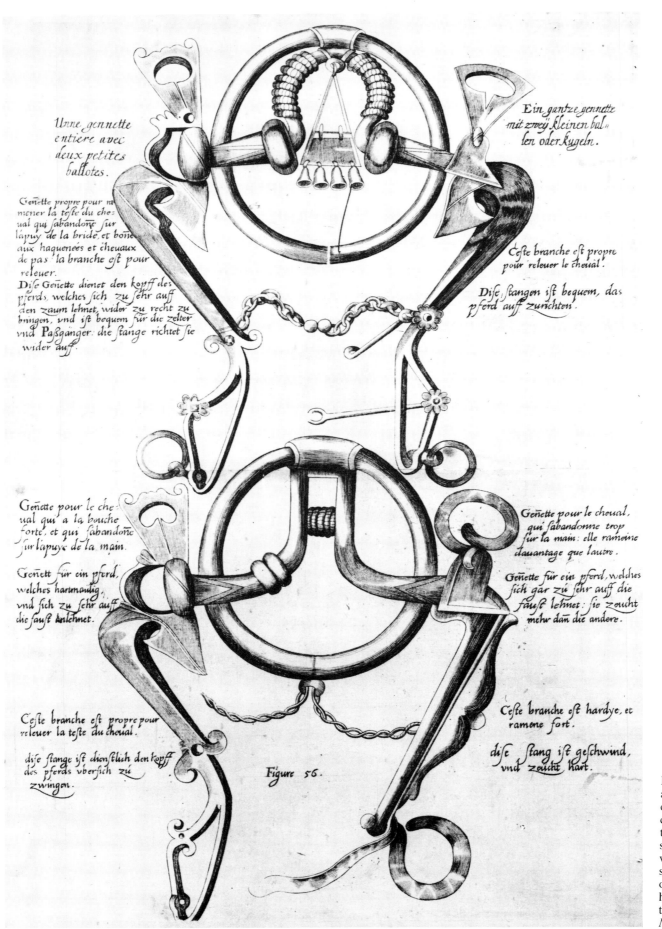

Unne gennette entiere avec deux petites ballotes.

Genette propre pour mener la teste du cheual qui sabandone sur lapuy de la bride, et bone aux haquenées et cheuaux de pas la branche est pour releuer.

Dise Genette dienet den kopff des pferds, welches sich zu sehr auff den zaum lehnet, wider zu recht zu bringen, vnd ist bequem für die zelter vnd Paßgänger: die stange richtet sie wider auff.

Ein gantze gennette mit zwey kleinen bulen oder kugeln.

Ceste branche est propre pour releuer le cheual.

Dise stangen ist bequem, das pferd auff zurichten.

Genette pour le cheual qui a la bouche forte, et qui sabandone sur lapuye de la main.

Genett für ein pferd, welches hartmaulig, vnd sich zu sehr auff die faust lehnet.

Genette pour le cheual, qui sabandonne trop sur la main: elle rameine dauantage que lautre.

Genette für ein pferd, welches sich gar zu sehr auff die faust lehnet: sie zeucht mehr dan die andere.

Ceste branche est propre pour releuer la teste du cheual.

dise stange ist dienstlich den kopff des pferds vbersich zu zwingen.

Figure 56.

Ceste branche est hardye, et ramene fort.

dise stang ist geschwind, vnd zeucht hart.

Here, too, there appears no shortage of variety of bit construction, for on the one page something like four varieties of curb are shown – but these are only intended for hard-mouthed horses that pull. From *Manège du Roi*.

62

Pluvinel on the Barbary Bonite, showing both rider and horse in perfect harmony. Lithograph by Charles Aubrys, 1833.

The royal riding pupil executing a *capriole* in the pillars before
members of the court. Copper engraving from *Manège du Roi*.

The Duke demonstrates a *croupade* with a left-hand pivot – an artist's idealization, quite agreeable to look at, but undoubtedly much less amusing for the ill-treated horse.

In exile in France and the Netherlands the Englishman William Cavendish, Duke of Newcastle, devoted himself to his own method of training School horses. He is supposed to have invented the *cavesson* and, by means of a special running rein, broken in his horses by forcing their necks to arch sharply on the spot and in small, tight circles. Such practices were handed on by him to his contemporaries and posterity in a magnificent work, *New Methods of Breaking in Horses*, richly illustrated by one of Rubens's pupils, Abraham van Diepenbeecke, but Cavendish won few friends for dressage riding by the book in his own country.

In a great apotheosis occupying two folio pages, the Duke of Newcastle is watched by a semicircle of his horses squatting in reverence on their hindquarters, as he rides to the ancient heaven of the gods on a winged horse.

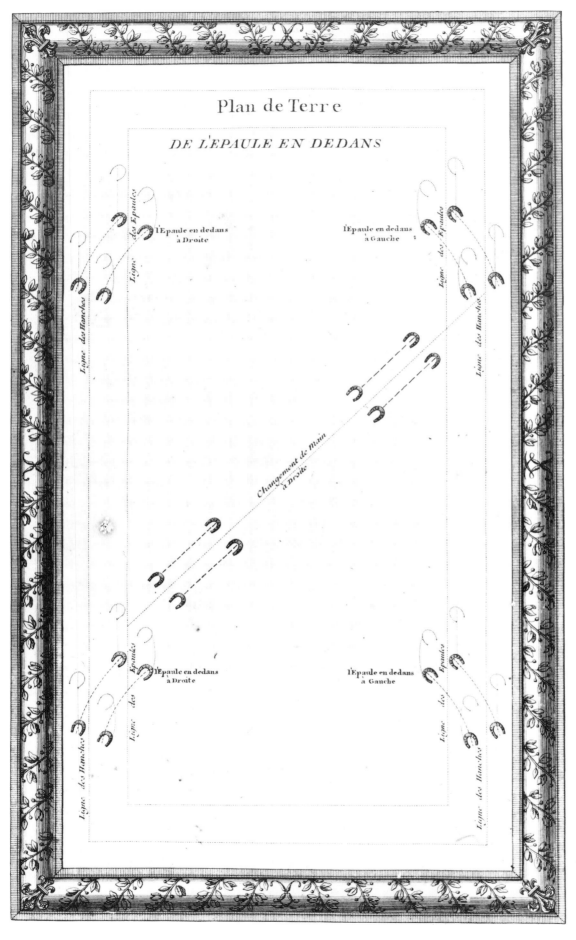

Plan de Terre

DE L'EPAULE EN DEDANS

l'Epaule en dedans à Droite

l'Epaule en dedans à Gauche

Ligne des Epaules

Ligne des Epaules

Ligne des Hanches

Ligne des Hanches

Changement de main à Droite

l'Epaule en dedans à Droite

l'Epaule en dedans à Gauche

Ligne des Epaules

Ligne des Epaules

Ligne des Hanches

Ligne des Hanches

In France the art of horsemanship, introduced by Pluvinel, progressed in the eighteenth century until it reached the peak which is now accepted as classic horsemanship. François Robichon de la Guérinière, instructor in a Paris riding academy, and from 1730 until his death in 1751 Equerry at the Tuileries, was the greatest reformer, critically considering every opinion he could get, and exposing and rejecting prejudice and error and all methods involving force. He laid the foundations of a special, well-thought-out system of teaching, based on knowledge and built up logically. He restored minor details to their proper perspective, introduced the 'shoulder in,' and cleverly applied advanced School instruction to the training of war-horses. In 1733 he made his knowledge and experience available to the entire riding world in his book *L'École de Cavalerie*, wonderfully illustrated with drawings and engravings by Charles Parrocel. The essense of Guérinière's teaching has lasted through the centuries and still serves as the guiding principle for the training of School horses in the Spanish Riding School in Vienna.

Side-steps, half-passes, hand changes, and turns are illustrated by choreography in *L'École de Cavalerie*. The plan of the 'shoulder in.'

The Winter Riding School in the Hofburg

There is documentary evidence of the existence in the sixteenth century, first of an open exercising ground, the "Rosstumblplatz," and later of a covered wooden riding hall, "Die Spainische Reithsall," in the ancient Burggarten, almost on the same spot where the Winter Riding School stands today. Then Emperor Charles VI, in the carefree days after the repulse of the Turks, ordered that a new riding school, providing shelter even in winter, should be built in the centre of Vienna between the Josefsplatz and the Michaelerplatz. The magnificent design drawn up by Fischer von Erlach was carried out between 1729 and 1735.

An equestrian statue stands as a monument to the *haute école* immediately opposite the main entrance to the Hofburg. The noble cavalier Prince Eugène, riding a Lipizzaner stallion in a majestic *levade*, is mounted high above the Heldenplatz. The memorial to the defeat of the Turks is by Anton Fernkorn.

The ground floor of the National Library in the Josefsplatz originally housed the Hofreitschule. The splendid façade has noble proportions, and the quadriga on the gable is a reminder of its original function.

The exterior of the Winter Riding School in the north wing of the Hofburg, with the Poseidon fountain, introduced later, at the north-west corner. The massive but well-proportioned exterior looks imposing from the Michaelerplatz, but gives little idea of the remarkable splendour of the interior.

An exquisitely drawn perspective of the Riding School building in its earliest days suggests better the interior brilliance of this great baroque creation. In the foreground is the ceremonial *carrousel* of ladies' carriages on January 2nd, 1743, with the Empress Maria Theresia in the centre, returning to the Burg.

In the open rotunda under the Michaelerkuppel, on the north carriage-drive of the Hofburg, is the visitors' entrance to the Winter Riding School. The striking architecture drives away banal, everyday thoughts.

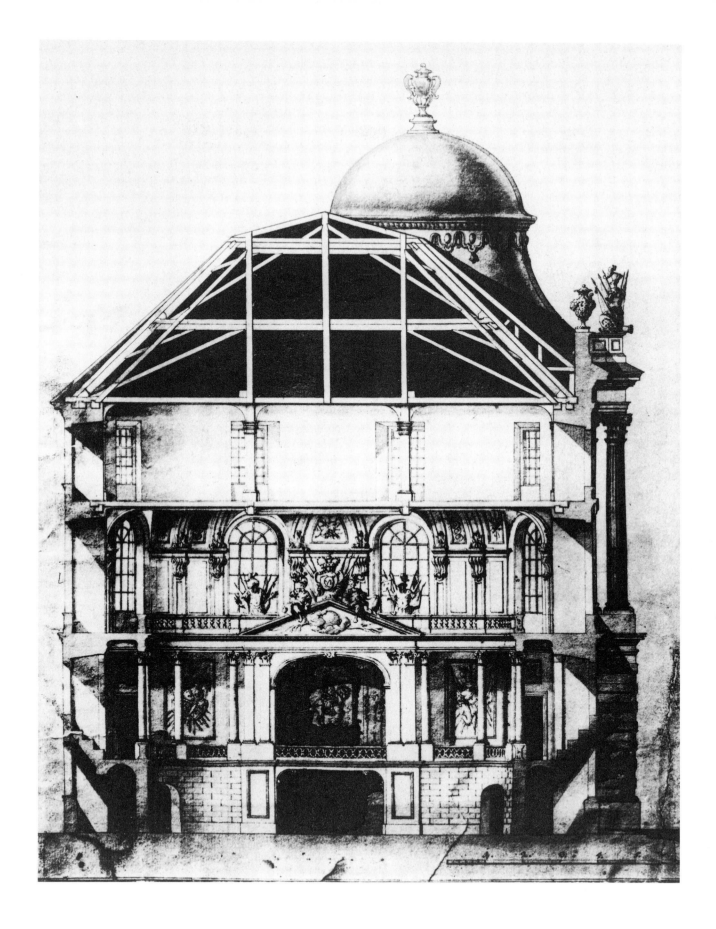

A sketch of the Riding School from the master hand of its creator provides an informative glimpse of the bold construction of the enormous building.

The Winter Riding School of Josef Emanuel Fischer von Erlach – the most magnificent riding hall in the world, a veritable temple of the art of horsemanship!

The light-flooded hall has a rectangular riding arena measuring 18 by 55 metres. Fifty-four noble stallions from Lipizza could display their artistic skill for the first time on September 14th, 1735, before their Imperial Majesties and many members of the Court.

Charles VI in a knightly pose on a Lipizzaner stallion – the equestrian portrait of the imperial builder provides the only colour seen from the front of the boxes.

At one time in this brilliant arena fantastic and lavishly arranged games on horseback took place, and *carrousels* of horses and carriages were organized, as well as many other festivities in the grand manner. Splendid balls, colourful masquerades of extravagant brilliance, and music festivals of the highest order were held here – and it seems as if the whispering and tinkling sounds still linger in the hall. There is an atmosphere of history, too, within these walls, for it was in Fischer von Erlach's building, after the stormys days of 1848, that the new Austrian Parliament met for its first sessions.

The inaugural ceremony of the first Austrian Reichstag in the Winter Riding School on July 22nd, 1848.

The Winter Riding School as a temple of music: in 1814 Ludwig van Beethoven conducted a mass concert here with more than 1000 musicians and singers.

Carrousel of twenty-four cavaliers in 1814. Contemporary coloured engraving.

The Ladies' Carrousel on January 2nd, 1743.
After the painting by Meytens in Schloss Schönbrunn.

Bridle, Saddle, and Spurs

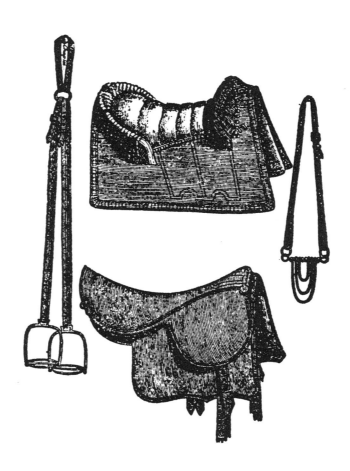

As the tools are, so is the work – the mentality of the rider is revealed in his equipment.

The change in the attitude of man toward the horse at the various stages in the development of horsemanship is also reflected in the rider's appliances, in the simple or ingenious, brutal or elegant fashioning of his equipment. In the historic collection of the Spanish Riding School in Vienna are all kinds of devices which have never been used there, although in general use in other old schools and which, in spite of their elegant shape, immediately betray their cruel purpose.

What might perhaps seem to be merely fantastic images on paper in the thick folios of Grisone and Newcastle are here preserved and displayed in some rare old examples. Spurs with shanks nine inches long! Also skilfully fashioned gold spurs that must once have given many a noble horse very rough treatment.

95

The show-case is full of stirrup irons in heavy cast iron or fashioned by skilled smiths in precious metals, useful and ornamental, and collected from the most diverse periods and regions.

96

Curb bits as used by the old masters.

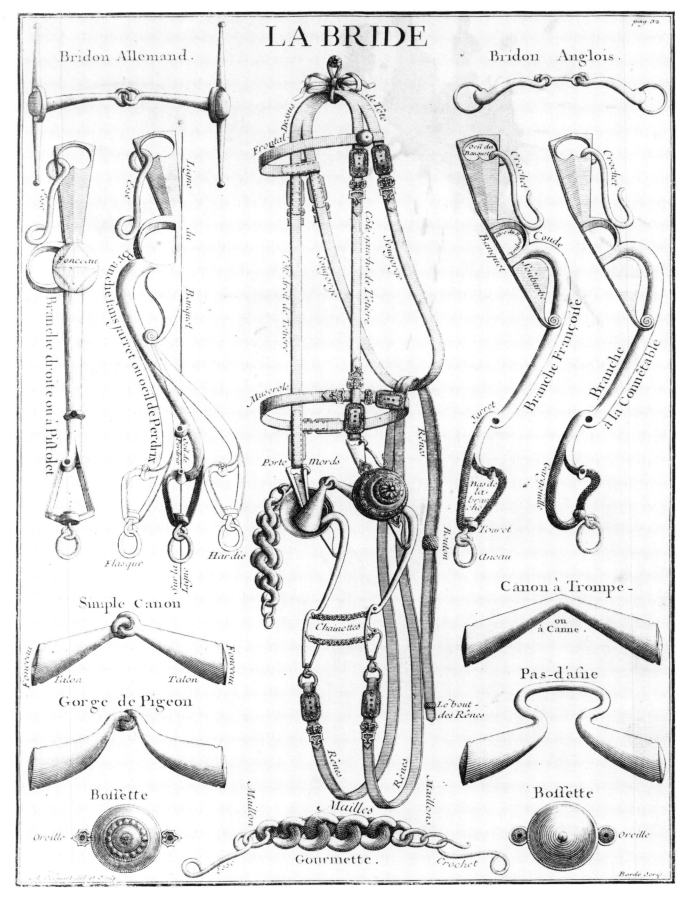

Always a great reformer, Guérinère, in his endless search for simpler working methods, omitted a number of complicated bit constructions from his textbook of instruction. He describes only some basic designs and only few variations, and warns against the sharp instruments still customary in his day.

A plate illustrating bridles, from *L'École de Cavalerie*.

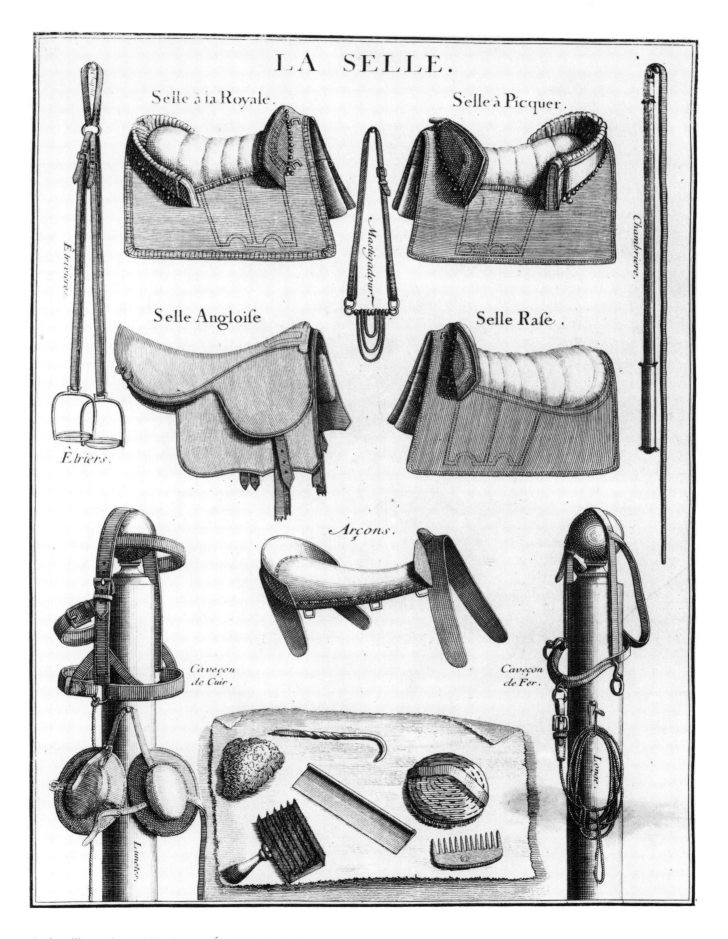

A plate illustrating saddles from *L'École de Cavalerie*.

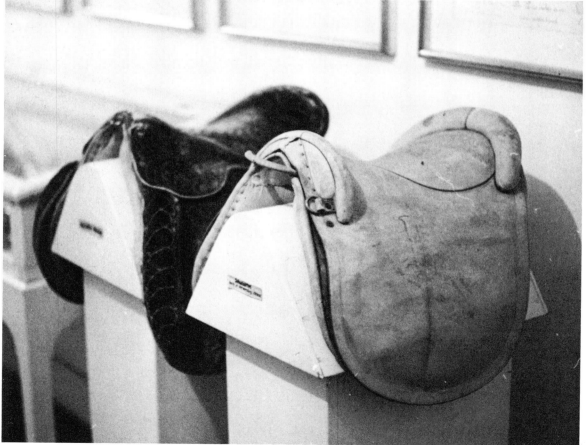

It looks rather strange today, but was very decorative and handsome. There were various intermediate stages before the evolution of the plain functional model that has been in use unchanged for more than eighty years – for daily work a saddle of newer English design is used.

The *cavesson* is often used for lunging and "Work in Hand", and also serves daily for leading the horses into the Riding School.

The snaffle bridle in red and gold used for display work on long reins seems to have an almost Oriental splendour. It suits its wearer, Siglavy Monterosa, superbly.

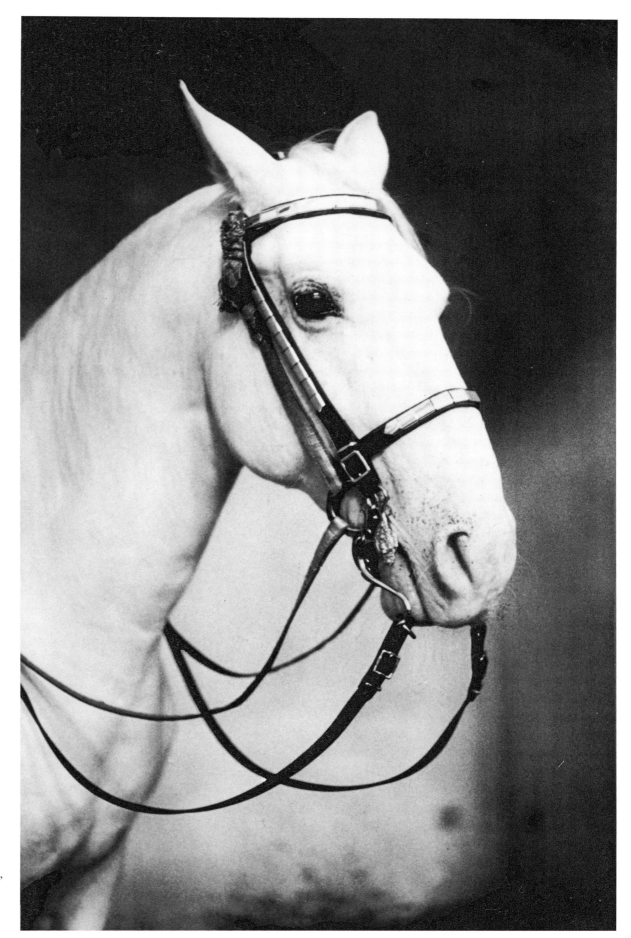

The gala bridle, used for
special festival performances,
has ornate gold decoration.
Maestoso Alea is self-
possessed and conscious of
his dignity.

The *Wischzaum*, or snaffle, is used throughout the young stallion's training until he becomes a fully-fledged School horse.

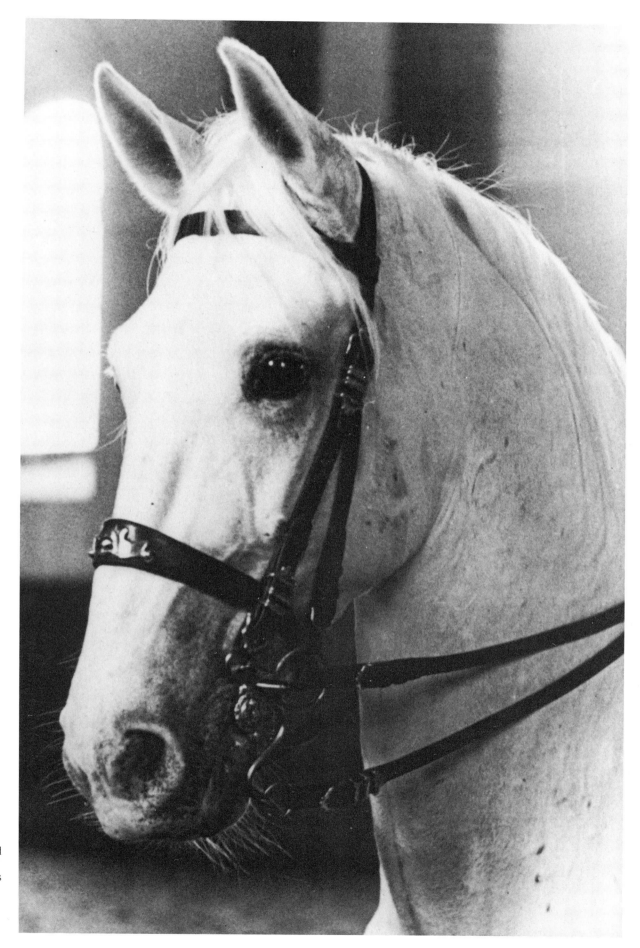

The discreetly decorated curb or double bridle of the trained stallion looks most distinguished. Pluto Theodorosta wears it here with obvious pride.

The Haute École of the Stallions

Today the Spanish Riding School in Vienna represents, as it has done since its foundation nearly four hundred years ago, the oldest riding academy in the world, and the only home of classic horsemanship where the teaching of the old masters from Xenophon to Guérinière has been kept alive.

Strict house rules through the years have united the training personnel into a loyal community.

By good fortune the directors of the School have always been men whose ability and personality have enabled them to cherish and preserve the traditional heritage of equestrian culture entrusted to them.
Until very recently the principles and methods of the Spanish Riding School training were handed on by word of mouth from generation to generation.

Colonel Alois Podhajsky discusses the objects of training with his personnel, and gives individual instruction for future work.

When they come from the stud to the School the young stallions are worked only on the lunging rein for the first few months, so that they may learn to trust their trainers and be obedient.

When first ridden the young stallions are taught only to go forward eagerly, and to understand their riders' directions.

Side-steps and half-
passes are used as
training progresses to
increase suppleness and
stabilize balance.

When the young stallion has found his balance carrying a rider he is carefully introduced to galloping work.

Unceasing faith in his rider is the best proof of correct preliminary training.

Passage, halber Travers links.

Like the old masters, the Viennese painter Ludwig Koch has portrayed in his famous textbook of instruction, *Reitkunst im Bild*, the various movements of the *passage* as they can be seen in daily practice.

The *levade* is an introduction to the "Airs above the Ground,"
which has also been portrayed in a figurine by Augarten, the
Viennese porcelain factory.

Spanische Reitschule

The co-operation of a second riding-master is often
needed for the first attempts at School leaps.

The *piaffe* in the pillars serves to perfect this exercise, but the instructor needs great patience and understanding.

Work is over for today.

Even dismissal is carried out in a traditional manner.

Pluto Theodorosta takes the sugar he loves from his
rider's hand after a morning's work.

126

During the annual holiday the stallions are walked and trotted in the Summer Riding School in the centre of the Hofburg.

Riders of the Budapest Spanish Riding School, which was founded in 1934 with its own stock of Lipizzaner stallions on the Vienna model, and was destroyed in the fighting at the end of World War II.

The Lipizzaner in Exile

In March 1945, a few weeks before the end of the War, the Spanish Riding School, with men, horses, and equipment, left its home in Vienna, which was threatened by air raids and the nearness of the Front. It reached Upper Austria and found in St Martin im Innkreis a modest but hospitable refuge for the uncertain period that lay ahead. It was the beginning of a ten-year exile!

A fateful hour soon struck for the School. In a hastily improvised, but completely successful, performance the noble white stallions introduced themselves to the Commander of the advancing United States Third Army. General George S. Patton, Jr, a chivalrous horseman, at once placed the School under the protection of his troops and, in order to ensure the survival of the institution for the future, had the Lipizzaner stud, which had been transferred to Czech territory during the War, brought immediately back to Austria.

The mares back home from Hostau do not have a bad
life for the time being under attentive eyes in
Wimsbach.

134

General George S. Patton, Jr, who took an active part in the first Olympic Riding Games in Stockholm in 1912, passes into the history of the Spanish Riding School as an understanding and resolute helper in critical days. Portrait by Boleslaw J. Czedekowski.

Olympic riders face to face: Colonel Podhajsky requests and receives from General Patton the protection of the United States Army after the historic performance in St Martin on May 7th, 1945.

A refuge in the last chaotic days of the War, St Martin can hardly provide the space and quiet needed afterwards for training riders and horses in the *haute école*. So the Spanish Riding School, in order to be able to fulfil its traditional duty in the future without interruption or restriction, moves over to the old Dragoon Barracks in Wels, where a regular course of training can be undertaken, and public performances soon begin again.

Spared by a miracle from bomb damage, the deserted Winter Riding School in Vienna was used for years as a scenery storage depot by the National Theatre.

His Majesty in exile: Neapolitano Africa

The White Stallions on their Travels

Because it was so secluded in exile, and there was no hope of a speedy return to Vienna, the standing and function of the School might well have been impaired had not numerous invitations to festival tours taken the Lipizzaner out into the world. These journeys, often to far-away places, demanded from the horses and their masters a very high degree of concentration and effort. Triumphant success was their reward, and world-wide recognition the result of their labour.

In Salzburg, where the Lipizzaner between the World Wars gave convincing proof of their skill in the tasteful setting of the old archiepiscopal Felsenreitschule, on their yearly visits from 1950 to 1955 they transform even a prosaic football ground into a romantic and enchanting dance floor.

The School shows its gala programme at the 1948 Concours Hippique in Thun in gratitude for the generous charity which in the years of desperate want has been given to Austrian children by the Swiss cantons.

The international indoor competition in Dortmund attracted a record attendance in 1953 and 1954 because of the performances of the white horses from Austria.

1951. In the intimate atmosphere of the royal riding hall in Christiansborg Castle in Copenhagen the ballet of the stallions arouses attentive admiration in the illustrious company of expert guests.

Ceremonial file-past before the stands at Aachen in 1953. Here, too, the Lipizzaner had already won great fame between the Wars.

In the vast football stadium in Stockholm in 1952 Neapolitano Santuzza excels before dozens of photographers and many fascinated spectators as a perfect *caprioleur*.

The School quadrille also enchants many thousands in Stockholm in 1952.

In 1950 riders and horses go on a long journey to the United States for competitions in Harrisburg and New York, to offer their thanks in the homeland of their protector, General Patton, whose great help has not been forgotten. Afterwards they pay a visit to Canada

Preparations for the performances in Toronto. The Lipizzaner are not at all upset by the unaccustomed technical factory equipment in the tournament hall.

The entrance of the cavalcade is illuminated by floodlights, and provides an unusual contrast.

Picked out by the spotlights, Favory Calais is poised for several moments in an effective *ballotade*, standing out strangely against the dark background of the vast hall.

A special performance for fifty Press photographers. Untroubled by the flashes of light all round him, Siglavy Bresovica in an apparently weightless *courbette* displays the power and grace of the trained School stallion.

In the Old World, as well as across the ocean, the precise figures of the great School quadrille always exert their irresistible charm.

In 1954 the Lipizzaner have unparalleled successes in the land of their forefathers, displaying their classic skill in places where normally the bloody spectacle of bullfighting sends crowds into ecstasies.

The festival appearance of the Lipizzaner at the White City in 1953 gave lasting encouragement to dressage riding in England.

In the huge arena in Seville several white stallions in the cultivated paces and turns of the *haute école* dominate the vast space and are given a great ovation by 20,000 spectators.

In 1958 the Spanish Riding School, in its first appearance abroad since its joyful return home to Vienna, brings the Concours Hippique International of the "Grüne Woche" in the newly erected Deutschlandhall in Berlin to a splendid climax.

Back at last in Vienna

Ten long years in exile have given the living community of the Spanish Riding School a severe test of its inner resolution and its permanence as a cultural institution. That it has emerged intact from all the struggles of those years has been proved ever since the day, so long and earnestly awaited, when the School was able to return to Vienna after the conclusion of the Austrian treaty.

A great moment. At a special performance on October 26th, 1955, Colonel Podhajsky announces to the Austrian Federal Republic the return of the Spanish Riding School to its original home in Vienna.

Before the brilliance of the gala première comes the quiet work behind the scenes. Also indispensable for perfecting skill in *haute école* technique are the riding lessons, stable duty, and care of equipment.

The lofty saddle room in the Stallburg contain, in exemplary order and arrangement, almost priceless treasures.

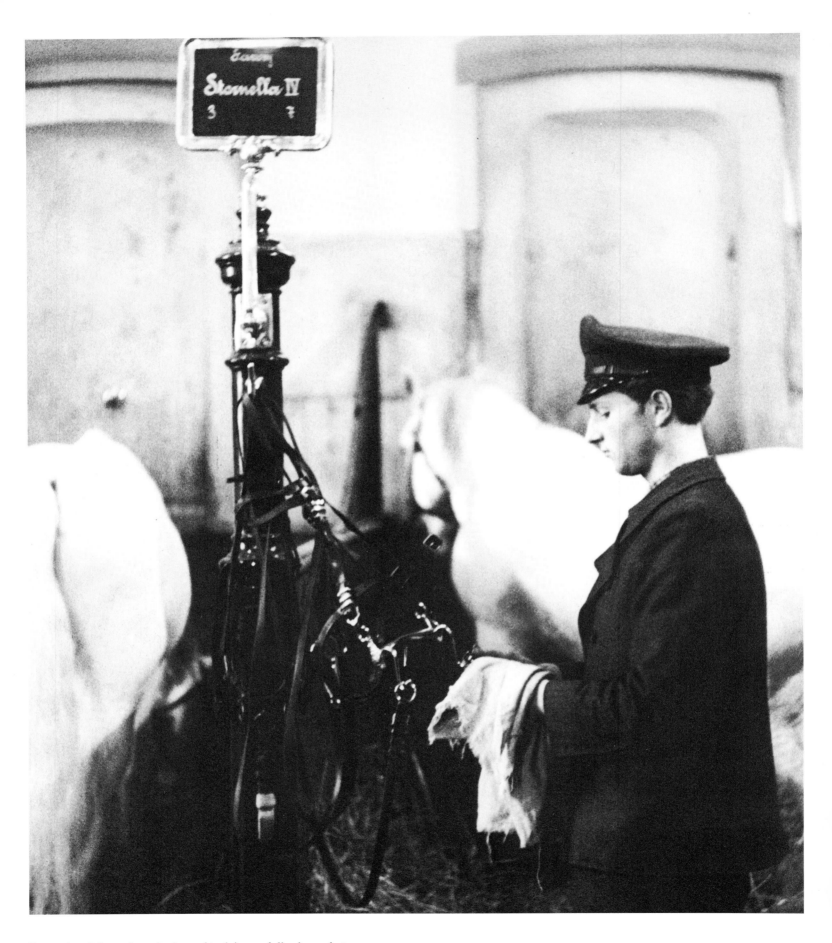

Every time it is used, each piece of tack is carefully cleaned at once.

160

Polished saddles and bridles for all the stallions are kept in
spotless condition in their proper places, and always ready for
use.

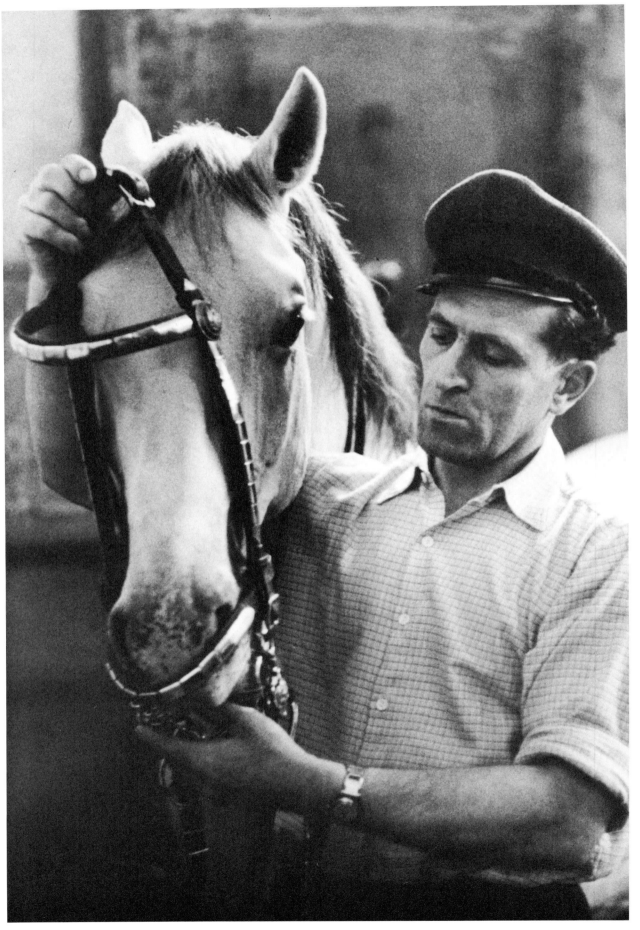

Every aspect of the care of the horses follows tried and trusted rules.

Putting on the bridle with a practised hand. There are no head-shy stallions here.

162

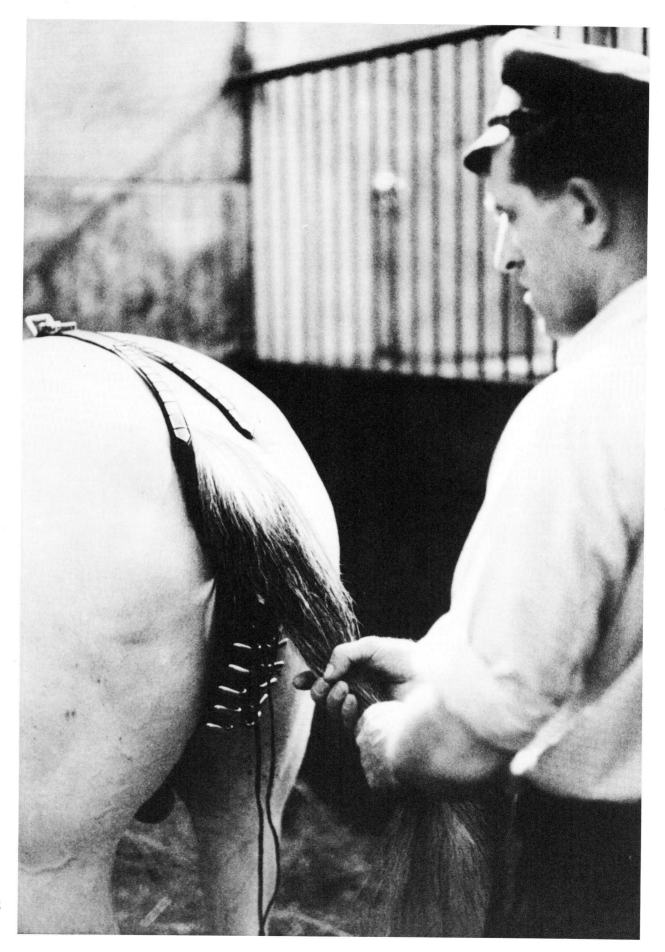

For the *capriole* the stallion, as in the days of the old masters, has his long tail bound into a leather tail-bag.

Even the riding pupils are taught to look after the valuable tack.

The historic uniform
of the riding-master
has a quiet elegance
unsurpassed in cut,
colour, and detail.

Even the awning
under which the
stallions are led from
the Stallburg to the
Winter Riding
School during the
winter months is
colourful and
decorative.

The stallions wait
patiently in the bays
of the *Pferde-gang*
beside the Riding
School.

167

Pictures and programmes of performances, and pieces of gala saddlery and tack, attract the attention of passers-by on their way from the Josefsplatz to the Michaelerplatz.

169

While outside long queues still crowd past the box office, the galleries of the Winter Riding School are already filled with visitors in party mood. Those who have been clever enough, or lucky enough, to get a reserved seat in front of the ornate fireplace of the Kobel box can relax as they wait for the performance to begin.

Prominent Visitors from all over the World

Since its return to Vienna the "Spanische" has been the objective not only of countless lovers of horses, riding, and beauty, but of prominent visitors and official guests of Austria who also make the riding academy an essential part of their itinerary.

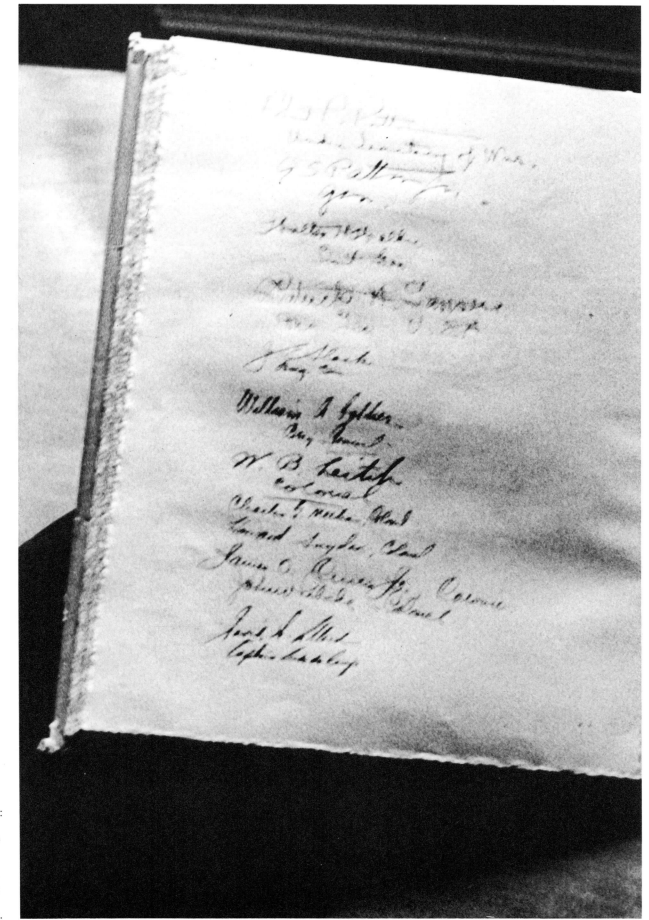

The Guest Book of the Spanish Riding School reflects contemporary history. An important document: the visitors to the historic performance in St Martin on May 7th, 1945, have signed their names – the second signature is that of General George S. Patton, Jr.

There is an atmosphere of cordial international understanding in the reception rooms of the Spanish Riding School.

King Bhumibol Adulyadej and Queen Sirikit of Thailand listen attentively to Colonel Alois Podhajsky.

Queen Juliana of the Netherlands does not want to miss a gala performance by the Spanish Riding School during her State visit to Austria in 1962.

Graciously following tradition, Queen Fabiola of Belgium signs the guest book of the Spanish Riding School.

Mrs. Indira Gandhi, then Prime Minister of India, enjoys a
peaceful moment in the busy programme of her state visit in
1971.

King Gustav Adolf VI of Sweden, ruler of the country in which the first riding Olympics took place, and himself a promoter of the sport, talks knowledgeably about horsemanship with Colonel Alois Podhajsky.

Dr Konrad Adenauer, Chancellor of the German Federal Republic, is so fascinated by the dance of the white stallions that during his official visit to Vienna in 1957 he asks for a special festive appearance of the Spanish Riding School in Berlin.

182

For Queen Margrethe II of Denmark, the performance of the Spanish Riding School is one of the highlights of her state visit to Austria.

A passionate rider himself, King Hussein of Jordan is looking forward with interest to the performance given in his honour.

Then the First Lady of the United States, Jacqueline Kennedy, a keen follower of riding, has a strong feeling for the clever horses [1961].

In 1953, Queen Elizabeth II had admired the performance of the Spanish Riding School in London. Now the Queen and Prince Philip come to see it in the magnificent Riding Hall of the Imperial Palace in Vienna.

Following his father, King Gustav Adolf and his grandfather, King Gustav VI Adolf, King Carl XVI Gustaf and Queen Silvia are the third generation of the Swedish royal family to visit the Spanish Riding School.

The American film actor Robert Taylor, star of the Lipizzaner film *The Miracle of the White Stallions* [British title, *The Flight of the White Stallions*], says goodbye after his first meeting with his fellow-actors.

President Ronald Reagan is presented with a Lipizzaner stallion to mark the occasion of the visit of the Spanish Riding School to the U.S.A. in 1982.

Exhibitions of Classical Horsemanship: Part II

Artistic enjoyment of the haute école is by no means an exclusive privilege of politically or socially prominent people. The Spanish Riding School is close to the heart of everyone in the land as a special cultural institution of the Austrian nation. It conquered the world on its festival tours, and today it enjoys unusual popularity in its home in Vienna, as is proved by the ever-rising numbers of visitors who come to the performances.

Three magnificent crystal chandeliers, carefully taken down towards the end of the War, and walled up to keep them safe from unauthorized hands, once more provide a glittering decoration for the ceiling of the Winter Riding School.

Colonel Alois Podhajsky on the world-famous Pluto Theodorosta, among his riders. Their salute is by tradition directed towards the portrait of the imperial architect of the School in the State Box above.

The performances begin with the young stallions and all the paces and turns of the *haute école* and, after "Work in Hand" and the "Airs above the Ground," end with the School quadrille.

When the truly majestic Maestoso Alea, or the exceptionally musically gifted Maestoso Mercurio, is ridden in time to the music of a lively 'galop' and rhythmic trot, changing from a perfect *collection* to an extended trot, in sidesteps and half-passes, in the School lessons of the *piaffe*, *passage*, and *pirouette*, the performance moves towards its climax in a display of classic horsemanship.

193

Neapolitano Santuzza, urged on by his teacher, shows a
model *ballotade* – the first step to the *capriole*.

The *capriole* in hand.

Ballotades and *caprioles* alternate, to the great delight of the enthusiastic spectators.

Bereiter Lauscha demonstrates a *courbette* on Siglavy Morella.

The Miracle
of The White Stallions

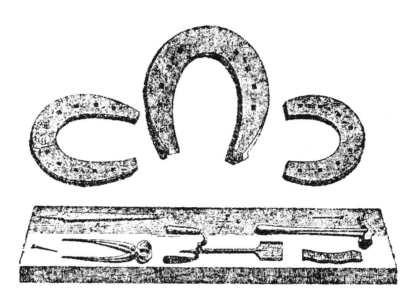

Siglavy Monterosa, led by Oberbereiter Irbinger, appears on
long reins in magnificent red and gold gala trappings, and
executes the *passage* as precisely as under a rider, also the
piaffe and the other exercises of the *haute école*.

The great School quadrille for eight or twelve riders is in a sense a monument to the fully trained School horse. The white stallions with their brown-coated riders never fail to enchant the spectators – whether in a balanced half-pass, a double 'shoulder in' on the centre line, or the so-called cross figure.

216

For the filming of *The Miracles of the White Stallions* [British title, *The Flight of the White Stallions*] Walt Disney gave the great School quadrille special glamour by re-introducing the old gala uniforms, which were last worn in the Riding Hall in the Josefsplatz in 1925.

Every Sunday the performances of classic horsemanship in the Winter Riding School in Vienna end with the great dancing ballet of the stallions. They recall a great age whose artistic spirit still lives and is preserved in the Spanish Riding School.

224